By June Gould

Scott Foresman
is an imprint of

Glenview, Illinois • Boston, Massachusetts • Chandler, Arizona •
Upper Saddle River, New Jersey

A police car helps.

A fire truck helps.

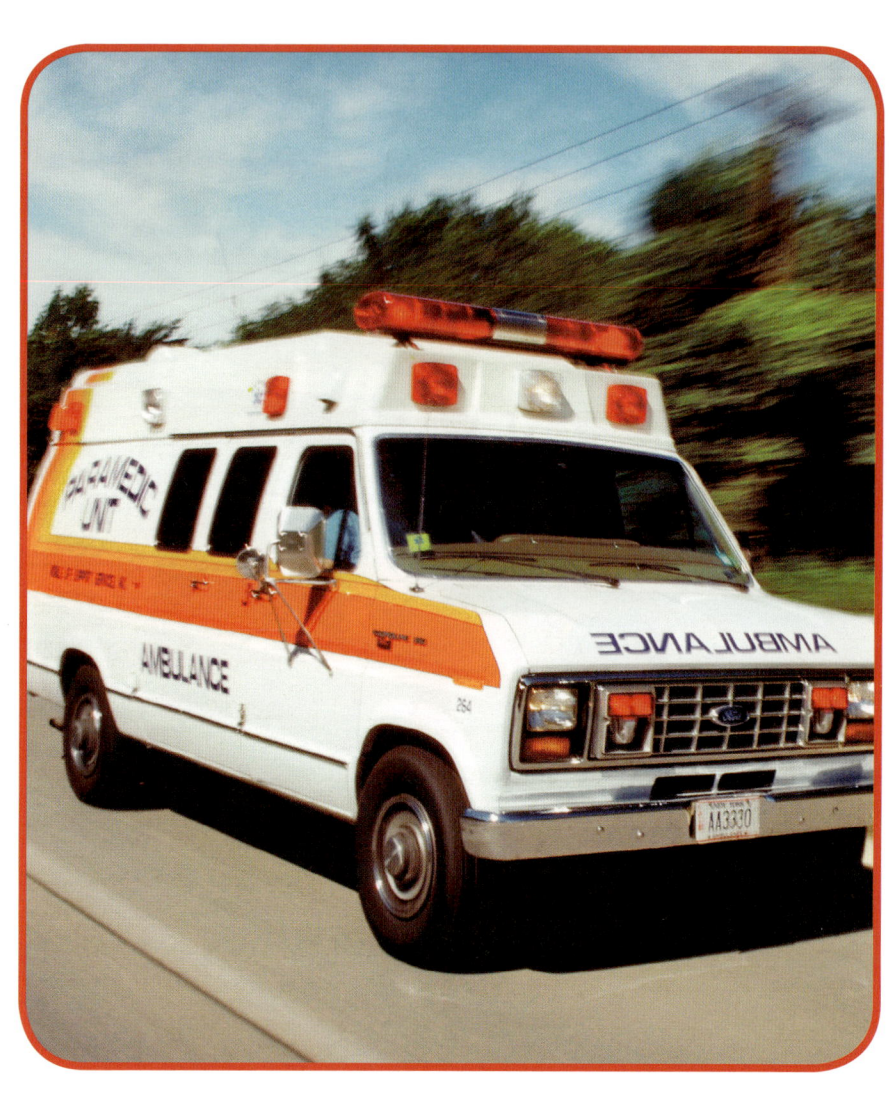

An ambulance helps.

A helicopter helps.

A boat helps.

A tow truck helps.

A motorcycle helps.